Poetry:

A New Definition of Life

Meltez Smith

Poetry: A New Definition of Life
Copyright © 2021 by Meltez Smith

All rights reserved. No part of this publication may be reproduced, distributed, or transmitted in any form or by any means, including photocopying, recording, or other electronic or mechanical methods, without the prior written permission of the author, except in the case of brief quotations embodied in critical reviews and certain other non-commercial uses permitted by copyright law.

ISBN
978-1-956529-02-9 (Paperback)
978-1-956529-01-2 (eBook)

Table of Contents

Family A Bond Forever 1
Beholding Others Fate 2
Belief In My God I Value... 3
Change Only A God Could Bring 4
A Great Influence.. 5
A Most Heartfelt Desire 6
A Fantasy Of Dreams!!.. 7
A God To Be Adored 8
A Human Beings Common Worth 9
A Love Never To Be Forgotten 10
A Mockery Of One To Be..11
A Tribute To Honor Father's 13
A Tribute To Honor Mothers 14
Ambitious Through Persuasion 15
An Evolution To Peace 16
Be Mines Forever 17
Everyone Treat Equal 18
An Undying Kinship 19
Confidence In What You Believe 20
Decisions Of A Lifetime... 21
Deliverance Only A God Can Give... 22

Earnest Blessed Prayer	23
Expired Time	24
Even Sad Times Can Bring Joy	25
Family A Bond Forever	26
Family Reunions Are Everyday	27
Familys How Together They Thrive	28
Farewell	29
Final Wish	30
Flight From The Name Saying Accusers	31
Freedom A Never Ending Battle	32
Gliss And Glamour	33
Friendship What It Means	34
God Simply Be Inspired	35
Humans Are People	36
Humility A Daily Statement	37
I Am My Brothers Keeper	38
Identify	39
In Justice Do You Prevail	40
Intimacy And Love	41
Let not Your Standards Dismiss Good Men	42
Liars Are All The Same	43
Life As We Know It	44
Make Me Yours Oh God	45
Marriage The Honor of a Lifetime	46
More To Know	47
My Burning Desire	48
MY REASON	49
Nature Our Key Example	50

Never To Be Broken	51
Never To Be Held Down	52
No Fear In God	53
No Rest For The Weary	54
One Day The Pain Will Be Over	55
One Day To Live In Peace	56
Our Fight will be remembered	57
Our Life A Mirror To Us	58
Pain And Pleasure	59
Plain Are The Words Of Life	60
Poetry A Life Art We Live By	61
Protected Is Our Deepest Importance	62
Pushing Through Adversity	63
Pushing Through Stress	64
Quiting is not an option	65
Races Of People Are No Such Thing	66
Remember To Forgive	67
Romance	68
Safety In Peace	69
Sin We Must Put To Death	70
Standing Alone Amidst The Rule Of Another Race	71
Standing To Not Be Moved	72
The Queen In A Woman	73
The All People's Club	74
The Journey of Faith Driven People	75
The Old Are Not To Be Pittied	76
The Rise Of A Princess Turned Into A Queen	77
Though Coming From Nothing Yet Always Great	78

Time And The Human Advancement 79
TRUE LOVE FOUND 81
Unspoken Voices From The Darkest Of Races 82
World's Greatest Gift LOVE 83
Where Faith Resides 84
Your Beliefs Are Not All Mine 85
Your Encouragement Is Life To Me 86
The Essence Of Love 87
Money Defines not Greatness 88
One God Eternally Great Forever 89
Make Life To Be The Most You Can 90
No Other Like You 91
Never Dought Speak Positive 92
Show Love Regardless Of What You Contend With 93

Family A Bond Forever
By: Meltez Smith

Family ties are so amazing blood is truly thicker than water. What can ever make me challenge the fate of my son and daughter

Why do you help your family when help they don't give back. Some answers don't make sense, but love will not tolerate lack

When do you draw the line, when do you mark the spot? With us why don't you dine, and see that memories are not?

Actions that you divide, with distance you keep quiet. From your family you have taken a denial adopted diet

What a phrase of words your cowards and wimps. Turning your back on your family, you hesitate with a limp

I guess if your family will kill you then by all means stay away

If you are worried about stealing don't be the fool to pay

For when you die just think who will remember me best

Mother Daddy sister brother, kids cousins niece and nephew

Tear this love apart and remember who it was left you…

Beholding Others Fate

By: Meltez Smith

Surrendering facts of my life to share, experiences I wish for no one to dare, cross by your heart or even swear

For I am a just living injust around much corruption seen in its lust

The day of deliverance may God we trust, the battle is won no need to fuss

Put down or conform to envy us, and endure what is hate put plain a must

For the true living God bring all your trust, til the day we unfold become the dust

Reigning in victory is seen our God, the mighty and powerful terrible God…

Belief In My God I Value

By: Meltez Smith

I am now to believe

From the past I fix my course indeed

Where troubles of shame come forth and bleed

And sorrows a flame that burns in greed, I know I came from life to lead

I know I shall in God believe

For whereto I go my end to be

Fixed and thus settled by a righteous decree

I am to believe for his favor is free

Success is the grand tour of life formed in he

Change Only A God Could Bring
By: Meltez Smith

Still I come mixed with the love of peace
Divide my some for to rest in peace
That my life be straight found in the best of form
To forever see the great from the cold world held warm
This is life I state before the heart fainted spirit
Clothe our mind keep our faith before your eyes do we fear it
Let our voice be heard and drawn in expectation
Take note of every word with our ears anticipating
We wait with love and kindness speak and your words are felt
We are led by sin through blindness fill us and we
are kept…

A Great Influence
By: Meltez Smith

I love the words of my gifted poems. Of the past and present uplifted they form. Entrapping words of guilt held to my face is all they be. To the light and point I stand to tilt, and expose the faces you see all held in me. Straight from the hell you see. A journey my hands can't free. Say what you will say what you please. A judge you place yourself stands not to confront these. Of trials and burdens I've felt yet the worst to what degrees. Your life is smooth and kept in a manner you so do please. But to abhor all those who hurt paying no mind to those who's lost. The value of your life you come to birth. Dwells in the small deeds dealt upon this earth.

A Most Heartfelt Desire
By: Meltez Smith

As we look out before us, seeing the best in what we long to be. Crying out loud is a begging of the truth. Screaming to be heard come a great destiny. Unspoken is not a word, found upon what we declare a plea. Viscious to the point where we will burn, to see our dreams be free. We dwell in tomorrow that brings today's victories. Always in the future do we attain today's joy. Having presently strong faith, is how we can boast with such victories. As a seemingly childish act we play with the future as a toy. Excelling to see the advancement in more. We push with all effort as never before. Being bound by great extremes yet we still come to soar, and the reward of our perseverance is the peace we live for…

A Fantasy Of Dreams!!
By: Meltez Smith

In my fantasy world dreams are big, no matter the sexes toupe or wig

Entirely limitless as desires I frame to be met as a reminder on the wall of fame

A reality getaway from society a stranger

A vacation trouble free where no host are in danger

A solitude of peace where positivity dwells

No greater person will succeed or fail

Blessed with ingenuity we face a nation that's intolerable of discrimination and it's place

Where all people are equal no big I's and little you's, will be our leaders of examples as we sit and watch from the pues

Competitions no such thing why compete when we gain

The praise of our wonderful teamwork is all we need to name

This fantasy do you like? Maybe or maybe not

As citizens we must fight to never lose what we got

The freedom to be what we want in our desire of God given rights

Let no man ever claim the decisions of your might…

A God To Be Adored
By: Meltez Smith

Lifted on high mighty exalted above themes

Where the great to weary cry be in our midst oh mighty of kings

Lord to your praise doth heaven sing, and heard from my mouth your praise to bring

Teach me Lord how to make your word real

Real in my heart to bow and kneel

As problems arise in faith yield

To rejoice and be glad you created me still

Blessed is this chance to seek your face

Unworthy am I to live in your grace

To you oh God I submit my will

Before the pleasure of your grace, and the last breath I yield…

A Human Beings Common Worth
By: Meltez Smith

Write and talk so eloquent
Be confident and strong as an elephant
Lost in a world of elegance
With a great demeanor of benevolance
What is my culture and background
And because of it why do you judge
Don't think that I do not act sound
Tradition of a racists is grudge
Your formal to those you like
But in your eyes I see much spite
Take that attitude for a hike
And don't let it ever enter your sight
For many we are who accuse
Few we are who agree
With this accusation we abuse
An opinion that should wait to forsee
The actions of people will tell more than they say
Not race or religion for free minds choose today

A Love Never To Be Forgotten
By: Meltez Smith

Loving me then loving me when. Effects of our help through trials blend. Poetically spoke your love's a gift. Seen to be a blessing come by so swift. Learned to be a lesson to aim and hit. The goal of acceptance to find and fit. I love you now and after death. I leave with you that memory kept. For we and all have our disputes. That last for a moment to peace salute. And admire it's change forgiveness here. Will let new life form and come appear. The healing process God speeds my dear. Thank God for love by his grace with cheer. We share the same love come know now here…

A Mockery Of One To Be

By: Meltez Smith

Seen in grief seen in class even seen in the best of my works, yet I knew in time you'd ask where are the beginnings of your works

To look in failure upon me you stare as the enemy of which I don't know

Your words mean nothing nor are they felt to declare any truth in my business you won't show

You don't know who I am you don't know how I feel, and what you think has no meaningful point

Because you fail to address and you fail to deal with every situation I try to appoint

What negative intent is your hearts demand as words to curse is your offer

Count all my losses to number them as the sand and a mirror for you is my offer

Attest this now and be a witness to my claim, no individual burden has entitled my name

To a problem incomplete only solved by the willing, your incompetence has made you afraid

To impart the truth and stand up and start dealing with your peers who love you and won't trade

Your personality for this situation obsurd you are company appreciated and so true

How can I phrase it or should I reword these valid points I must do

To amend my ways and seek better ones to follow with aggressiveness preferred change is recommended

As I sit and write and feel empty and hollow this smile never dies nor have I hid it

However seen may I be known for peace besides the many faces I disguise

For to love and enter his face so sweet is the dream I pray be the skies…

A Tribute To Honor Father's
By: Meltez Smith

The day of Fathers or Fathers day
It always bothers me to say
In a very good way you have set the tone
In providing plenty you are king and known
Seeing your great example of the lead role you took
Now we form a sample to the great cause we look
For upon this day holds all dignified men
This where true love lay for our Fathers win
Every time you hear and behold respect
Before his face you fear his words never neglect
Of our love so true in your arms we feel
Like a kid showing off of his great fathers skill…

A Tribute To Honor Mothers

By: Meltez Smith

Mother's day is a reflective day as a woman's work is not done

In the month of may, may I love you more even when our time is all done

Such hands of love that have kept me warm

Such great concern that led you to warn

Mixed the pot of fear on my butt you've torn

Did the best you can from the day I was born

To whatever mom in whatever state

Thought of very fond to your child you're great

Just remember this you'll always be here

On our heart to list cherished memories dear...

Ambitious Through Persuasion
By: Meltez Smith

Touching and amongst this visions reach. Unfolding at large power to speak. Watching each day like a movie script. Surrounded by negative people who afflict. A race to survive and prepare for the worst. A great uneasy drive is a debt from a curse, but now is your time and the calling to hear. God's grace shed so divine to impart wisdom here. As truth comes we align as his power now shapes. To your glory Lord do I find peace in all of its wake…

An Evolution To Peace

By: Meltez Smith

And When we allow freedom of joy to commence
Look upon all people around love build a fence
Then dwells inner strength where gain is seen to promote
The attributes of love is there through any tide remaining a float
An equal balance together where you and I are strong
It doesn't matter to whoever this is the example and model of the strong
Where time and centuries have endured much wrong
We define new efforts in our future they belong
Give outstanding ovations to dreams not seen as a loan
For off in the air they fly to a destiny set in our minds we have flown
And captured all that is set to be the remaining endeavors we free
All held under one rule we see his name is GOD forever with me…

Be Mines Forever

By: Meltez Smith

Standing before my eyes so bright with a beautiful ray. Who else could it be my love and dream to stay. Witness the enchantment of a bond so ever to be close. So long as we're alive this love must constantly roast. Everydays a new and every minute is a lesson. May you come home safe is what I think when you are dressing. My tender baby wrap me in your arms. So much love and passion I wish it could grow on farms. May joy and gladness be the meet of our after life. I would be so privileged for you to be my wife. From walks in the park I put my head on you and cry. And I am not ashamed nor am I even shy. Disputes in the court they say opposites attract. I count it a blessing that our love is a fact. Know me to the heart and know me to the core. As tears from my face just ever drop to the floor. You are my love in your pretty eyes I am lost. A fool that lays his hands on you does'nt even know the cost. This precious woman draped in perfumes of flower. Grab my hands and step aboard as this love of eternity towers...

Everyone Treat Equal
By: Meltez Smith

Respect of all is the creed I live by
Remember me as the one who always let you try
To be who you are in front of me, and never put on a face
Despite however you look, you are a person in my face
For who am I to look down on any, or offer some disgrace
No fortune in the world against this demeanor, could misplace
The value of human kindness and it does not mean being a loser
But when this value is ignored you have become a user
That's right and abuser, who considers others as trash
Sweep and walk all over people but in the end you will crash
For nobles and earnest people who seek to do well
You are the contrary and I promise you will fail…

An Undying Kinship
By: Meltez Smith

Here we are a family gathered here today.
Well most of us at least for the best I can say

For a special occasion you can believe.
May be a birthday, wedding or a time to grieve

It's a very sad thing when we don't see each other often.
As grave attitudes arise from the stinch of a coffin

We must learn to let differences from the past remain.
For the love we have who can maintain

From the ones we've seen and grown to know.
Whose beauty within we love to show

As tears of love flow down from our face.
Who will we let to our families disgrace

From something that's planted in us so deep.
From good intentions it comes to leap

In front of our families who can defeat

What toleration of love will let you take a seat

For your family of whom you suffer with long

Beside the point of even when their wrong

The undying love we must let none replace

As our attitudes we keep of love to abase…

Confidence In What You Believe
By: Meltez Smith

There is no stand I seek to make
There is no faith I see in vain
All dreams before me has come to wake
While my conscious beliefs are known by name
To escape the past from filth I came
Wondering so blind by sin I blame
But glory to God who for love has slain
Abolishing sin to hide no more in shame
Nothing's redundant when I praise his name
You can change with the times and keep with man
For the Lord holds the signs with eternity in hand...

Decisions Of A Lifetime
By: Meltez Smith

A treasure you hide of importance you keep,
of malice and guile you don't offer to speak

And yet so serious for yourself is true,
for you exactly apply what you say to do

A prefect man you can never find,
a breech of contract is your word you have signed

Your word is your bond to which you are held,
an option thrown away in scenarios we have failed

Structure is gone whatever you say it can mean,
if up is down then red is green

Some can kill and be off the hook,
others can do it and your body they'll cook

Justify who they want condemn who they wish,
don't give a second thought the next day go and fish

So many talked of hard times to come,
a day when people offend to have fun

I used to think how worse could it get,
if any disagrees I'll place you a bet

For the news is tramatic and our lives are the same

A monster of rage everyday I must tame

Still I love life and for nothing will I trade

But the freedom we have will it diminish or fade…

Deliverance Only A God Can Give

By: Meltez Smith

*Holding on with a grip that's fainting
I'm guided by signs always seen*

Ever looking hopeful with my status ranking among the lowest degree ever felt and seen

But God's peace I find in the encouragement gave. Where a day of promise is mines and the Lord God shall save. From iniquity shown he reigns! understanding of his will all supplied. In the day when my struggles held all my pains. He stood right there never left my side, and now in him forever I humbly reside. Where the chosen few dare in ridicule never hide. To the righteousness before our God his word remains to never lied

In the city of the upright called are the few he will hide

And preserve to the very end all the glory and praise we shall give

To our master Lord and king we send, the greatest treasure ever known to men…

Your Praise"

Earnest Blessed Prayer
By: Meltez Smith

Thank you Lord for your guiding hand that protects me all through the day

Not knowing where I go or where I sleep unto your spirit help me obey

I love you lord but don't know how to yield

Please with your grace teach me how

To come out of sin as in truth I build

With an unworthy demeanor I bow

And close my eyes while upon you I think

Many tears come flow from my hurt

Of your blessed comfort what have I to think

God considers me and I am dirt…

Expired Time
By: Meltez Smith

On this blessed day I've come to declare
And make known what's obvious among many
The life we live and the life of despair
It totals not few or many
Being held down in bondage so to speak
With confidence laying heavy in the balance
And a horrible day for me to show and speak
And express abroad unseen talents
With a grievous mind that's led by hate
For the cause of which your going through
Others can't imagine or even escape
Let them talk for they'll never be you
Trials are great and rewards are too
For the meaning of your life is grand
Take and see what lies of you
And declare that time is at hand…

Even Sad Times Can Bring Joy

By: Meltez Smith

It's in times like these I write my best. Through sad teary eyed feelings I can't seem to get a rest. Will I ever accomplish what I'm trying to seek. My dreams and visions seem fadingly weak. I tell myself this is just a phase. Through my eyes alone I must amaze. To enthuse myself to stay on the right track. For I can't stop now or even look back. How grim it is to go through what I am. As situations put me in an tighter jam. I try to break free as power moves I make. That seem to be drowning in a never ending lake. But perseverance is an option of must to take me through whatever. This aweful life that dreads me to mourn when problems are going away never. To keep that bold and swelling desire to let nothing stand in your way. For whatever you put your mind to you can do more than speak to say. To prove to unbelieveing eyes that actions are louder than words. To always stay watchful and leary, as shepards of flocks of herds. To be so noble and earnest in contending for what you hold dear. To make your words be plain and simple even if they cause a tear. To give every person the benefit of respect that all men deserve. Respect not contigent upon race or possessions for our lives we cannot preserve. To be so thoughtful and helpful of those in dieing needs. To not be so self centered to make good deeds unfreed. To be so willing to follow and not always take the lead. To be patient enough to understand before quick judgement will speed. To say what is only needful in keeping feelings in mind. To watch and guard your tongue that only you can bind. To always strive for the best in everything that you do. To remember as long as you live each day you see is new…

Family A Bond Forever
By: Meltez Smith

Family ties are so amazing blood is truly thicker than water. What can ever make me challenge the fate of my son and daughter

Why do you help your family when help they don't give back. Some answers don't make sense, but love will not tolerate lack

When do you draw *the line,* when do you mark the spot? With us why don't you dine, and see that memories are not?

Actions that you divide, with distance you keep quiet. From your family you have taken a denial adopted diet

What a phrase of words your cowards and wimps. Turning your back on your family, you hesitate with a limp

I guess if your family will kill you then by all means stay away

If you are worried about stealing don't be the fool to pay

For when you die just think who will remember me best

Mother Daddy sister brother, kids cousins niece and nephew

Tear this love apart and remember who it was left you…

Family Reunions Are Everyday

By: Meltez Smith

We dwell in safety where we fear no more, and the troubles of our past are done

Yes another fantasy I adore that shows the true meaning of fun

We eat and play and laugh and sing, and the harmony of this is peace

We go beyond our time to bring whatever necessities are no lease

Keeping in touch and sending letters as well, we have many forms to show our love

Blessings are much from which we can tell this family is truly of love

Our disagreements never keep us away, and no trials are to great or strong

This is the unity to dream and pray, and the fellowship of a family that's grown...

Familys How Together They Thrive

By: Meltez Smith

Familys are so controversy as we see each other often.
Burdened by tensions and emotions that soften.

It's sad when special occasions bring us together. With heart feeling love that can't seem to be touched with a feather

Why do the ones closest hurt you so much. The words you say to me in what way do they touch

We as a family need to examine our actions. Come to a common solution that will solve these fractions

No longer can we deal with spite among each other. For when we hurt our loved ones its us who truly suffer

In considering a major nessecity allow me to stress this last point

A family must stay fit connected to the body as each joint

For we are one in many members that play an important role

Love and embrace your family until God rest your soul

Farewell
By: Meltez Smith

Be home and at rest
I hate to see you go
Admiring your best
With memories I know
Live on live on
Inside of me
Through flesh and bone
I weep with thee
Cross my hands
And close my eyes
And visit other lands
Where my dream belies
I'll miss you deep
While thoughts I'll embrace
And cherish to keep
Alive the sight of your face…

Final Wish
By: Meltez Smith

Dance for me and sing this song.
For in that day when my time has come.
A legend in disguise be gone.
May the joy of my gladness have come.
In what I see to behold this man.
With evidence unsighted from many.
You come to me and you come to hand.
Respect that I ask from plenty.
So seasoned much with tasty flavors.
The recipe has already been fixed.
And it's so polite with natural favors.
It's me with an abundance not mixed.
To laugh and cry let you stand by.
In the lines of those to be met.
So words of me will be no lie.
And missing you my only regret…

Flight From The Name Saying Accusers
By: Meltez Smith

I fled to see burdens take flight
Been dead to the dreams now in light
Be found and known by the dreams you possess
Be found on a throne to govern themes we infest
Among the simple to complex, the chains of our lives being put to test
With degrees of our talents unseen to bless
Offer no hate for our skill is blessed
So I fled to learn all as an ordinary man
Being led and held captive by the goal I demand
To be spotted out like a star many light years away
Compare me to the life we are of indulgence and dismay
For the right I have to be free, and in your ear when I die
The greatest ones damned to believe in hate are the souls hell will fry…

Freedom A Never Ending Battle
By: Meltez Smith

We've come so very far and I have never seen. The slavery of my people the lifted their voice to sing

And you wonder why I get so furious when I'm in the midst of a racist

I don't care what you say, guard your hands and watch there places

For two strikes have already passed, the third you are presently at

You're walking on ground that's unsteady, for hating me because I'm black

Kill me so what I don't care, then it must be my time to go

Your devious acts are cursed and the memory of me will show

You hate humans that are not your color. A punk and a alien you are

To wimpish to fight like a man, and a stranger to the life we are

That makes us God living creatures for treatment of the same to all

It all comes back to pride, where great empires rise and fall

Gliss And Glamour

By: Meltez Smith

When I talk of gliss and glamour and behold sweet awesome dreams, when I tell you of the banner real Christians hold not in schemes

I point out to my desire then scream out in pain and weep I won't what I admire for I've never had my keep

Far before when I retire with bitter anger for a life I reap, Look at this pleasant smile evil ones just try to kill

Curse your grave and burn in style hateful words from one not ill, the sun yet shines again blessed mysteries behold ideas

Yet wondering in lust of sin I feel God say try his, look not and fore judge no end see the person you are and face

Each individual born into sin very few will change that face, for our lives are lit up in works, and our end is dressed to mourn

Selfish greed boast many works a normal disguise from life untorn, pictures of cries from those who've worn

The sweet blood stained banner of Jesus held partook of his manor and never fell

These are the few all blessed with grace, ridiculed and scorned but see his face

In a new life being born upon peace they trace, setteled in his way to not be displaced

So talk of the gliss glamoured in your way, expose the sins you've hammered today

The gliss and glamour all fade away, what is for certain is here to stay…

Friendship What It Means

By: Meltez Smith

Hey are you a stranger at all
Not a foe or loving kin but a friend I can call
A partner maybe suitable to be a husband or wife
Definitely unrefuttable is the trust of you with my life
You've come to my aid from what seems to be thin air

Unjudgemental and showed peace is laid, where there is forgiveness among all to share

Disimpart and break down to me friendship facts

We are the art of the town around here we impact

The seen of a love that never lacks with attitudes to relax

In calm words never sparing a smile we are true friends shown in acts

And what shall take our graceful legacy on to a level we are fit

Beyond the realms of normal people shown is you and I that's it…

God Simply Be Inspired

By: Meltez Smith

Come love see shout and adore of his goodness. You have no earthly idea about the greatness of his fulness

And this is to everyone you cannot fathom this power

With no endless bounds more than outrageous is his power

His wonderous magnificence is the key to a humble life

Denying ourselves daily caring for his word more than our life. God is our creator the one and only means of our survival

Putting him first and never later everyday we live is a new revival

Be honored greatly for the trials you suffer just like his son we must do the same

But remember in him was found no blame. Recognize in us is found all shame

Can't you see here this vivid picture, of just how meaningless and frail we are. I pray that one day his power hits ya

As a life of obedience to our God we are...

Humans Are People
By: Meltez Smith

He looks at me and she looks at me, and my history is but what I said

While they look they behold to see, such strength and valor is not dead

My skin is dark and I don't feel beneath, nor will I take my seat behind

Eat my steak and eat my beef, while I sit beside you I dine

Equate me with truth and equate me in peace

Let the morals of my deeds be defined

Or look at me strange while I look and feast

And bask in the freedom so defined

See I've had enough, and I've had it up to here

If you can't accept it then just dissappear

This is life of blazing colors

In everything around that you see

Accept all life with no rebuttal

No matter what color you see

Humility A Daily Statement

By: Meltez Smith

I humble myself before the proud I'm convicted
I look not to myself for it is God who's uplifted
My expressions behold the name of the one you see here
My reflections yet hold the same great old endeavors born to appear
Not in the form to scrape up a penny where you have seen my struggles laid
Right in the open and eyes of many I stood right there to divide what's made
Remembering the days in my car I PRAYED
And precious gifts I sold to trade
This day Lord when will it come to an end
Just to make my dividens sustain to ammed
The right place and order where I'm fit to win
The house seat and marriage was the choice and trend…

I Am My Brothers Keeper
By: Meltez Smith

Talk of poverty to end is to talk of good hearts in men
When finally selfish ways cease a new bridge is open to peace
With many exits from a world of pain
Yet so many choose to stay on that lane
The bigger and better picture of all people at large
To see leaders with a heart for people that take their seat in charge
Push the pride to the side
And be proud for what you don't hide
People will love you so much
For our lives you have touched with a clutch
Stand up and be so very different aren't you tired of seeing people in a rut
All of this money you have is it really going to be that much of a cut…

Identify
By: Meltez Smith

Not nearly spoke as a man not nearly seen as a woman

The role that held our greatest fan is seen now just as the woman

The backbone of our head the commanding role that we took

Has been stripped away and misled upon those who take the same look

An outcry bears upon vengeance for the fairness being dealt to our youth

They want a single mom and dad not a combination mixed in untruth

You say you're who you say you're what please say what you've been born to be

Never has there been any laughter of the matter when it comes to the person you see…

In Justice Do You Prevail
By: Meltez Smith

I'm few with words highly spoken in deeds
What I write shows verbs of the underlying man that bleeds
Oh no it's not blood and what you see is not a fool
Nor a temple of mud to be used like a school
Talk intelligent and smart or be quiet and leave
Let me be the start of what you see to believe
You expected and thought and you gave me no chance
Just admit your at fault or just remain in a trance
If you apologize learn more from what you did
Take time to execise equal rights that's not hid
Upon those you select who aren't worthy to recieve
The good benefits you except the bad ones you should grieve
For it's a very sad thing why your attitude should change
And very terrible what you bring to the ones you name
Experience is this from my words you hear
These lessons are list may you come to hear…

Intimacy And Love
By: Meltez Smith

Grab my hands and feel me close.
As my nerves react to your touch.
To this form of intimacy I do toast.
And bask in the enjoyment of such.
Yes it's sexual entertainment of love.
And you are the prize I behold.
With a mellow temper and beauty above.
No woman can ever take your hold.
Upon what you have upon this my dear.
Dwells deeper than what you see here.
And even after a night of pleasure.
Your words are important to my ear.
On my shoulder remorse is felt.
Through my words encouragement is gain.
Life and honor are held by the belt.
But my love is held by it's name…

Let not Your Standards Dismiss Good Men

By: Meltez Smith

Exchuse me oh Mrs. none approachable, is my swagger just much to different? Are my ways to antisocilable? just know that daring is the one to be different. As you caught me staring, step up right to the mirror. With a radiant glow all glaring I decide who is realer. Reflecting all that is bearing upon my mind like a dealer. Seeing the more than what your wearing my heart comes now as the thriller. Get to know this man for who he is categorized by his own. Let me have your hands just to kiss and your body on my throne. And not a word will I miss, let your wishes all be known. For the favors of my love is great, let me spoil you and enrich. Be the queen that I adore and mate, until my course of life then ends to switch. Be the chapter upon my life to create, the fire that gives me my glitch…

Liars Are All The Same
By: Meltez Smith

When you tell a lie false statements compound, as more and more they switch every time you turn around

But when we often hear them how upset and shocked we are, until you say a lie a joke that does'nt go far

Some of the biggest hypocrites yes I sometimes lie, like when it comes to who I am with this troubled mind you don't try

A white lie is considered not bad whoever heard of such a thing, if in my mind it is just don't step to my face and bring

An accusation of why there is no guilt for reason, it's always ok for everyone else to use the point of treason

And when I hear a lie to me it does the same, so who am I to put down for what I refuse to tame

Then you have the nerve to question me as lame, no answers will I offer from stupidity is where you came

Go ahead and be the saint falsify doctrines of truth, make up signs and tickets abroad an idiot is renting a booth

Let me set myself clear for the record lieing is in no way right, but those of you who have itching ears will hear my words as they bite

Feelings get hurt that I understand but we're playing the ways of the world, politicians and big names I speak have took the word lie for a twirl

So next time you hear a lie think about how many you've told

I promise the facts won't be perfect so remember what stance to uphold…

Life As We Know It
By: Meltez Smith

From the day we were born our future was unknown
With no choice in the matter yet time goes on
We see the finer things of life grasp hold to what we adore
As the hour glass of time yet continues to pour
Tears come to my eyes when I think how life is short
No man is strong enough to resist death as a fort
In spite of we live day to day oblivious of our end
With no remorse for our shameful deeds we are invisible as the wind
Yet we are blessed and favored for the morning will come soon
For those that live to see it and hear the wonderful tune
From birds chirping in the trees and wind blowing in the air
Some things are so priceless no expense would be fair
In this joy of life where the rich and poor clash
Celebrate your life's meaning before it's gone in a flash…

Make Me Yours Oh God

By: Meltez Smith

Lord God make my courage strong in spite of the eyes of my enemies
No man can endure troubles long instill your word within me
I do suffer and I have cried, but how could I get hell twice
The day approaches where many have died you don't have to gamble or think twice
But what I know is where I reside longing for what yet remains a mystery
For unto you what can I hide when the effects of my life is misery
Time does not stop nor will it pause but to the light Lord bring me
My faith and endeavor must never cause shadow of turning from thee
Before I die to never wake again let your truth be my life
Corruption is the heart of sin, but never must it be my life
For if my purpose was to be your pleasure teach me Lord to be just that
Nothing ever can mount to measure the satisfaction of your word…

Marriage The Honor of a Lifetime
By: Meltez Smith

To you I bewed with this ring I signify. Our life long commitment will not only simplify. These vowels to be taken through thick and thin we remain. No man can ever split what you desire to obtain. Through flesh and blood I have sweat. Through whelping tears I have cried. If only time would just let. My remorseful deeds that I hide. To be changed from my past so my future won't have to suffer. The consequences of my actions must steady yet make me tougher. For the both of us have failures, but together we can learn. Coming into this relationship has already caused a turn. In a new direction of faith, when all you can do is believe. To cast our nets of hope, and never look back to retrieve. Everyday is your will. Stop and think compromise. The heads of two must deal. In a fashion that will systemize. For marriage is such a great job that's rewarded when you learn. To deal with life as a couple and from each other never turn…

More To Know
By: Meltez Smith

Poetically spoke as rap not with a song or music to hear
With a purpose to come forth of my goal entrap
And bring to lights vision the form of a true tear
Made right before your eyes is a destiny set
Where words lift and come to rise equal on all levels met
To claim you know me all cut with lies
Everyone I deal with is in disgiuse
Faces are the many changes of approach
To this life a game and you are the coach
Dressed in all my sighted clothes you can define
Hate love or stay out of mine
Be a friend get acquainted and come now and dine
Where peace and harmony mix so much in line
And truth and grace sticks right here to find…

My Burning Desire
By: Meltez Smith

This illusion of a dream has captured my mind and trapped. Thoughts unable to immerse in this vision I have mapped. For the world to hear my writings with truth from the heart. To see a stand point of life that journey's from the start. In a wide variety of matters and behaviors overlooked. That go into an area of controversy in a record that is hooked. To give a different point of view, from the stance that I see. Listen to those accredited, but take my words to be. The definition of a man, with experience not much. That two eyes and a heart have touched many and such. Not to receive praise, but to tell life from my eyes. In riddles, rhymes and chants, so plain it unties. Adversities of life and better ways to deal. Like anyone with a degree, in life's problems are'nt real. In life lessons are a must when you talk what you know. Not any school can teach what the streets will show. For everything I write I have witnessed with these eyes. The windows to your soul are not gloomy when it tries. To block out what it sees when apparently it is wrong, and make up excuses, that won't last very long. A voice to be heard, standing with esteem. May the words of my mouth be acceptable to bring. Tears, joy, anger and peace. Emotions that envelope a perception to cease. Many thoughts of me will run through every mind. When you hear what I have wrote, a declaration to be signed. For in myself I don't glory but thanks be to God, and two ever loving parents who did not spare the rod. Please I humbly ask tell yourself you can. Succeed in every point of life for you are your biggest fan.

MY REASON
By: Meltez Smith

When I stand up and perform I love to cause a scene
Fill your head with knowledge and bring to life my dream
A poet of our time to not say I'm better than any
For true inspiration I've learned from the ones I've seen and many
To talk about the times wherein we dwell so people of all ages can relate
And respect the value in freedom of speech for this is the
remnant we create
Once this remnant is lost I fear we will no longer be free
But trapped in a mentality of a slave mind thanks to our leaders who see
No importance for us voicing our opinions don't ever take this for granted
The day will come when our future speaks of our children's
rights what will be granted…

Nature Our Key Example
By: Meltez Smith

Skies so blue grass so green.

On a beautiful day my heart can sing.

Of wonderful thoughts being caught up in the mood.

Nobody around to be so awefully rude.

This is a time when my spirit is at ease.

From life's everyday problems all I hear is the breeze.

Such a wonderful time to sit and reflect.

As my mind goes back to all I regret.

The warmth of the sun to the mosqitos that bite.

Accept the good against the bad we fight.

So much wisdom in little areas unknown.

We're caught up in ourselves like we sit on a throne.

Valuable lessons each day we miss.

Are as a vague expression of a thoughtless kiss.

Never To Be Broken
By: Meltez Smith

The humble are as grass though we are cut assert resilience, for to live by peace is said to have no class

And the justice of its unrighteousness is held intense, For the love peace and happiness we sent

Has the all we gave now been spent? to your conclusions ration make sense, make a love between us a fence

For you have your own mind and we have ours, enshrouded not in secrecy but liberally empowers

Proclaiming this belief held in its truth as it towers, God is our king may we praise you with showers

The blessing of hope rest in your name most holy power…

Never To Be Held Down
By: Meltez Smith

*As a pedestal anchors footsteps down in tears, by our jobs
they rank us underneath them in fears*

Scold and taint us to what appears

To be nothing but equality shown with cheers

A destiny for greatness is never viewed

From the eyes where you taste this is a wrong attitude

Just know that now we must not conclude

In the midst of your evil and despite your rude

The best yet to be seen and by our faith we are there

From all the joy you have stole no longer mounts to where we air

For peace sought to be whole is now the treasure that we bear

Toss our heads back held high receiving greatness from our Lord

Through the pity shame he held us high and mighty is our Lord

No Fear In God

By: Meltez Smith

Ready are the prepared and sworn are the committed
In the sky I have stared in the mirror I am fitted
Protected by my knowledge and fortified from within.
Trash talk is but garbage and silence is the end
For counter attacks to come evidence is for sure

With unseen mounting sums disaster and no cure

Unstoppable fate! deliverance is their any? Peace in God I state, with joy of ease there is plenty

Ready sworn protected, through great trials we are perfected
And though aliens to our present peers, the cause of greatness has our tears

Melting our hearts in gratitude humble faces do we carry. Through trials he trains our attitude

By the leading of his spirit we tarry

Ready sworn protected by, his grace may I be elected

To bear his cross with great grief, this trying journey is the last

With abundant words I do speak, to be with Jesus all I ask

No Rest For The Weary
By: Meltez Smith

Listen closely watch my eyes see the pain and hurt, caught up in many twisted lies with anger I dance and flirt

Call me what you will, lift no hands and be smart, in confrontation I don't deal and fights aren't fair if you start

Jealousy a strong rage money a strong passion, don't ever look at age don't ever look at fashion

Welcome to the grand life where enemies you watch close, forget them and a knife will stab you and your toast

Oh that's so harsh why do you talk that way? The streets is a marsh waiting for fools to play

In a game as old as time where winners are not any, you're on top for the moment you shine and yet you're worth less than a penny

I am sorry I give it to you raw for justice is not on our side, on your brain let this thaw in tears of disgrace I reside

From peaceful sleep I awake to another day unthought, where time must take away everything we have sought

In the years gone by and generations we've seen, our desires so high and our youth so mean

Vile is our society and immoral are our ways, not fit from sobriety in the event of what plays

In our economy that cost and to us never pays, this is a great lost and who is it that pays...

One Day The Pain Will Be Over
By: Meltez Smith

The hurt from pain is now obsolete. From continual torment it is now complete. As if hitting your hand with a hammer and nail, it becomes num eventually and you can't even tell. It's complete because in it you do not dwell, as whatever you're dealing with takes you through hell. You must realize what's at stake. Your life is so adoring, and not just for your sake. A unique individual a one of a kind. Does'nt matter what others say their not the only ones that shine. To put you underneath them and theirselves on a footstool. Want to make you feel like nothing, so you can see who's really cool. From such pay attention none for in secret do they deal. To satisfy their selfish minds against you they plot to kill. Oh what wills and thrills of joy as they long to be in charge. What passion of self motivation will consider your life at large? Driven to the impulses of insanity their moves who can call. Don't ever let them put you in a position to where they back you against a wall. The brain is the main power source from which direction is applied. We must keep emotions under control or what's next will fall beside. To feed off what you've given thought it will fuel the fire. As intensity grows within you your temper will rise even higher. We must take our minds away and off to see the big picture here. Don't let it make you feel like your hearts all filled with fear, because we must remember the pain is now complete. As veteran eyes do not waste the time in arguing to compete...

One Day To Live In Peace

By: Meltez Smith

Misfortune is grave and sad, but peace be yet with thee

Remember the good and bad your eyes are blessed to see

Greet me and be true agree not with my ways

Hold it not up to you to determine and limit my days

What is the price of life and the cost of it to keep, guard yourself and life and let all others reap

Keep your mind just set on whatever you intend to be, hold the power to get what freedom has reigned on thee

Live lust and adore in a reasonable manner that's good, ever hope for more to better the things you should

The possibilities are great though situations are many, act as a fisherman's bait and watch the joy of plenty

For everyday good and bad will rise be steady as they fluctuate, yes it's an uneasy task but on the goal you must punctuate

You're not in this alone with billions of others you share, a common ground of a struggle that yet just seems unfair

But with faith and grace we push in hope of a better day

Before our time has come may God please bless I pray…

Our Fight will be remembered
By: Meltez Smith

Beyond my reach is beyond the grave. Where no words can speak or come forth to save. From inevitable fate there dwells my class. Yes the ones who shape and dignify class. Who walk this earth in filth and rags. All seen from birth as invisible flags. We held our crown when shown no mercy. We never stayed down for success were thirsty. Being angels unheard of being angels never seen. Aggressive like I heard of the wolverine terribly mean. Stake our claim legends under God by his might. To walk among many edgeing out a traced map of our fight. To live in peace and whole pledging to see better days in our sight. And now we come from nothing and reign in the pleasure shown. By the blessed God be of Heaven we are seen now as the known...

Our Life A Mirror To Us

By: Meltez Smith

In the coming days for what turns to years, sat upon greatness of infallible tears

For to judge ones self is the light of truth, that burns from the innocense and childhood of our youth

Mocked by our change and solutions to excel, upholding the banner through great burdens we sale Lacking in much yet strong in spirit, as we brave the storm of the worst we fear it

As our captains before us sought gravely to clear it

Yet dealt in our hands are no morals for good. Evil and savage are the fruits of our good

To learn to see past the innate immoral man, and reach unto what we ask in forgiveness from every man

In the days when our love would bask and make even the coldest of hearts be grand…

Pain And Pleasure
By: Meltez Smith

What is pain without pleasure? On this wonderful topic I will lecture. Don't tell me grown men can't cry

Don't tell me it's ok for you to lie. Don't tell me you understand what I'm going through, but imagine and come close to wearing my shoe

Where feelings so harbored become expanded

Where good deeds you intend have not landed

Upon importance of life that's a must. To simply maintain and trust, in yourself to be more than a achiever

Despite the many words from a deciever

Maybe you are the head of your household, or wife as the title to behold, and the elderly and children of all ages

On this subject I could write many pages. For pleasure and pain is not the same to all. For who I like you would'nt think to even call

Tell me I'm ugly and I ignore. Tell someone else and see what's in store. It's important to sympathize with the way people feel

For pain without pleasure is very real. How long it will last who can ever know. The degrees of turmoil will eventually show

In stress illness or even death. To name a few but many are left. Never think people are weak because what they face

For each personality has its on taste. So to understand pain without pleasure

You must first understand a mans measure…

Plain Are The Words Of Life
By: Meltez Smith

Talk to me straight forward with versions of truth explained, don't even look fake towards opinions of dought unnamed

You see and you hear of intelligence standing right before your eyes

Speak in the state of benevolence understanding my features and size

Compared to no other in lies, declaring not my words unwise

And seeing earth's treasure this prize

In the day when kind people never dies

Speech the very aspect of language held with great power in its tongue

Joy and great turmoil of anguish spread to the detriment of some

Season your words with such caution as in the face of adversity being dead

Sale no pitch as an auction and rest every word to be said…

Poetry A Life Art We Live By
By: Meltez Smith

From Edgar Allen Poe to Langston Hughs and Maya Angelo.

Including the King Dr. Martin Luther a few of the poets I admire so.

Hear encouragement from our stories, poems we've lived and from our imagination.

Hear trials of conflicting worries, forms of our lives not found in encapsulation.

Don't honor me, But admire my work. Sit down and appreciate such language unheard.

That when I write for me it does a great work, to speak and be still known from the poems you've heard.

Excellence found not because a life of fame.

Mark me compared to many, but in heaven put not my name.

Judge me by the standard form, and leave my faith up to my God.

What I mean is the standard norm of todays form but peace I seek in God.

Protected Is Our Deepest Importance

By: Meltez Smith

Down from below instill encourage gain we must know
For peace we even show this is a life for the great to grow
From down below is where our treasures are hid
Not in the arrogant or mighty but from our troubled hearts we lived
Barely escaping the day of death
Blessings unfold when there's life from breath
Enhanced and untold are names we kept
Of those who loved us and for our burdens wept
Never knowing how we make it before our eyes seeing our dream
Before a crowd I will break it and let loose loud as I scream
Breaking all theories thought I come live and bring pain
Better now to bought in love is shown where I aim

Pushing Through Adversity
By: Meltez Smith

While some of my greatest work, has far yet to be seen and heard.

And paycheck to paycheck is dirt, that scrapes every penny with nerve.

Calling forth out of the mean, and unthoughtful day where we reside.

Are kind and sweet loving things, that most individuals do hide.

A personality so broad, and a fantasy so wild.

Forever life has just scarred, this good natured loving child.

But yet through my experience, some other one may be healed.

In particular my children, the future hope to be sealed.

For those who know me and those who don't, many faces they have seen.

A heart sweet angel and killer king, through time and patience inbetween.

Yet never have I renounced my faith, and curse my grave if I do.

Though a sinner I am safe in belief in God I am true…

Pushing Through Stress
By: Meltez Smith

Sitting and thinking and thinking and sitting, not enticed to start drinking, but find a way to keep from sinking

As I go through each day with a clueless mind, then fall asleep at night with stress all combined

This is life told so perplex where every situation is trying

With the Lords help I am next despite the facts I'm denying

In hearing my words faith is sought to flex with all the goals and plans supplying

The honest truth that is put to rest my dreams and calling from the hate

I lived a life that kept the records of my best by standard of living though late

Consumed the knowledge you hear I speak is all I ate

To mark the grand day I date

With hands uplifted praises in my mouth to shape

The joy from pain I now escape

Quiting is not an option

By: Meltez Smith

Though almost slipping yet through demand I grip
From sinking shame bound to the hills I rose
With an attitude cautious yet though unsteady I slip
For the trials before me was never my endeavor to be chose
Where the element of surprise leaves you in shock to be froze
Seen is the dream and the envision I pose
Supreme is my desire and determination my drive
Where we excel in what's higher we often fail in what we dive
Being head strong to not hear, an island not meeting any to compromise
We are what hell brings on its high end, and what grief lays in demise…

Races Of People Are No Such Thing
By: Meltez Smith

To all cultures of diversity spread is their reasoning within your mind

For all our hearts have been deceived and led to believe that we're one of a kind

Like a special breed that's the pick of the litter

We all bleed and neither one is fitter

Found in my mouth so bitter

The taste of a one classic hitter

Best of all in life we are bigger

Whatever color born we deliver

Traits and virtues we all share

Confront the enemy of division and despair

To walk freely towards regard and not spare

Be a new seed birthed and be fair

See people not color and be rare

Dwell in the highest achievement great

The love of all humanity found in shape

Remember To Forgive
By: Meltez Smith

*One voice to another echoes the great sought out redemption.
From far to near is our sequence set in stone*

*A trail of events that lead to our cause in redemption.
We were never born to be perfect, but so often are we not misunderstood*

For our lives are more than just worth it, when it mounts to the cause of our good. Seen as noble felt dead as wood, in retrospect to our intent

Call us lazy but never no good, for we hold in all our greatest intent. The negative that comes in our direction

Is yet the same that comes to all. The only difference being our confession never being to great to admit we fall

This is our inherentance to fall and rise, never giving in to the shame where we dwell

We seek abundance to the life we prize, As well as forgiveness through a life we trail…

Romance
By: Meltez Smith

Romance is the subject favored in what you like.
You are the subject of the one you've come to like.
Yes the main attraction don't ever take them for granted.

Behold the beauty fashioned upon love which has landed.
Through every extreme expanded

This king and queen forever banded.

Other found beauty cannot compare.

Or come close to put down the one true heir.

That walks as a song speaks like the wind. To one do they belong, firmly set courted upon this trend. That which is hoarded consumes the end. Failure abort it for love is kin. Mixed with the romance combined all in. Now tasting great is the life we share. To ever find common ground is two of a pair…

Safety In Peace
By: Meltez Smith

On my knees I drop to say please cover me oh shadow of mercy.

Hide my face from the one who sees and has the power to curse me.

I'm stricken with grief my sense of direction is gone, and worst of all what is my end to be?

I've talked with pastors and my counselors have known that I remain in this rut longing to be free.

No sleep at night I just lay in my bed this stress has taken over my whole life.

I just think I might live to get ahead before I lose everything including my wife.

I am a stranger from the everyday world we live I am a voice that speaks into the air.

My demeanor is unreal but respect I give for who cares about the load that I bear.

Yet and still this face just shines from the depths of my heart can you see.

Take and feel what I treasure is mines this is my gift to be free…

Sin We Must Put To Death
By: Meltez Smith

Your scale is tipping and it must hit bottom
From birth into existence is the death we find in autumn
This hour glass of time that no man can rewind
Enjoy the little time for our destinies are signed
Each person just so unique with our bad habits we long to kill
Every child born just oh so sweet forgetting our nature
to the sin we yield
That traps our mind daily always forced by our will
In the war against our flesh only few stand still
Breaking up our families and tearing us apart
Is the three corrupt word that dwells in our heart
This gene inside us all must be understood to ever change
Just as the first we all will fall but so the redeemed dwell
in his name…

Standing Alone Amidst The Rule Of Another Race

By: Meltez Smith

With dignity I stood, and still as the only black I stand. For the same job that is good for them I come to demand.

For equal rights in us is born, but as we grow not kept. My skin is dark and I've worn the coat of displeasure I felt.

Numerous times as my love just melts, yet anger and hate are not observed. When compassion is sought and you require my help remember to you my color is obsurd.

Not fit for peace and unheard. You don't like this so what I've been mad. Turned away from jobs broken hearted and sad.

Oh don't look sad you know why. I'm never qualified to even try. Any job that's more money than I need. Including anything that I can use to feed.

Racist are what keeps America under. Where to dream of unity is to wonder. If the generation that brings forth the younger.

Will also bring forth this wonder…

Standing To Not Be Moved
By: Meltez Smith

Its time to call out time to stand up and make a big deal
Commotion is much in where we stand to be devout
Upon our beliefs we strike no other for how they feel
We are the empire that brings peace still
Ever pushing our agenda is how we stand and never yield
Time brings a constant change yet how should our morals be defined
Evolving to what kind of state could morals advance the humankind
We will never settle to be changed for our beliefs can't be forced
Our intent is much enriched and framed with our beliefs
bravely voiced…

The Queen In A Woman
By: Meltez Smith

With love and grace does she walk. As her heart beats I stand at attention.

All night and day we ever love to talk. Even if I'm busy her sight commands my attention.

Mrs. Wonder of my dreams when will I find you. I know your out there waiting humbly for your bou.

All the while glad and eager, dreaming of our kids together.

To be found fit to meet her supplying her needs or whatever.

Knowing that on me she can just depend, and not in love alone.

For our hands intertwine and mend to show just one even tone.

Through disagreements we are never to be stuck on our own.

And I don't care how extreme our love is much to strong…

The All People's Club
By: Meltez Smith

In the all people's club you can be whoever you just wish, this is the equally same treated club the motto of all colors we don't dismiss

And neither do we flock to our own ethnic group, but in all jobs together we strengthen people as a group

For there is no majority race superiority we cast down

For simply all to know among this place a color issue is unfound

If one chooses to bring one up how we will miss you, and hope that through grace you are found

Supplying all of the people skills you will never be made

Every day is a joy that fills human kindness displayed

Unto all not just your race should this treatment be shared, can you form your mind to face such peace that's unspared

In dwell among us found true, and only look at those who oppose as strange

We are friends that invite you to the color of all people brought here to arrange

The all people's club where no race is rejected

The all people's club behold grace fill excepted…

The Journey of Faith Driven People
By: Meltez Smith

Tons and tons loaded with heavy persuasive views. Filled with none less, but abhorrent and tolerant news. Come stand to a week in fame. Not from the people, but the victories you gain, and let a week go forth to claim. Many months and years we remain the same. Through a hostile environment, the caged beast we tame. To confront our beliefs true, find the enemy be slain. In the light we impart to you, this integrity retain. For our mercy is fine but few, and with our courage we stand to remain. The sought out kings among the class of elite. Where from the heart truth rings, and to opposition comes defeat. When all around have fallen, we are found in our seat. With such a dignified faith and calling, we are found among the weak. And through our history known and spread is a legacy taught to fear. Before our grave last breath we led. Looking to the one and only God we fear...

The Old Are Not To Be Pittied
By: Meltez Smith

We've come to all our finished marks, we've come to see our end

Though old in age heart flames with sparks of courage and wisdom to share within

Beyond the ranks of untitled decisions, we bring to reality our fate

And let you be the judge of such blind decisions, for upon our experience is truth straight

Yet through your eyes are new faces witnessed, with valued opinions to stand guard

Along many choices detailed and finished, honest faith is upheld to be hard

Granted in peace supplied with favor, answers are not vague as they appear

For truth is laid right upon this table, cost of consequence must adhere

Either now or later what's done is revealed, and resentment to such judgement is unfair

For in time we see our debt unfilled, to our self or a host in the air…

The Rise Of A Princess Turned Into A Queen

By: Meltez Smith

There she is and there she stands. The woman that holds my love has my pleasure at every hand. Just say the word speak, and I'm at your feet. Come whisper in my ear with a voice so sweet. For you are the honored queen I behold as my bride. Only to you I trust and lean, forever love me never leave my side. As we go on journey of a renewed love ride. To ever leave me I would be hopeless standing still where I cried. Not a sensitive baby, but a man who knows a womans worth by what we confide. In the time you get to know this man. You find unparallel forms to the men you've tried. Let me cut this short for the point is reached. My love expands from the one seen here. You have the map to find all you seek. Touch and feel my heart now and release a tear...

Though Coming From Nothing Yet Always Great

By: Meltez Smith

Been looked upon with no pity great shame still staring at me

And the afterthought of did he mount to be what was said a decree

Now fate has chosen the form seen right here

Now you may fall in to where I disappear

From negative changes are choices made

In the midst he arranges the decisions played

Just never forseen was this amorous day

To whom shall be the queen is a dream I yet pray

For true love dwells in crossed right upon my heart

May she know where I've been lost in a world far apart

May the time come when I cast all my treasures

Right before your eyes I'm the one love measure…

Time And The Human Advancement
By: Meltez Smith

The sun has set the moon will rise.
Stars will fill the midnight skies.
Predators lurk in search of the weak.
Never unaware of what they seek.
Ever so brave each day more bold.
Life so quick your dear ones hold.
Time to sleep your body must rest.
Thieves will find a good home to nest.
Security alarms and guns at hand.
A map of entry to fit your land.
Regardless of just how prepared you are.
A persistent minds limits go far.
Hope for the best the worst expect.

What will the history of our time reflect.

Same blue sky same bright sun.

More cost to living a more advanced gun.

Death rate unspeakable national wars abroad.

Leaders that come to the front and lead the nation by fraud.

So much negative and not much good.

I only wish that people would.

A wish it is not ever to come true.

A wish it is for peace is through.

TRUE LOVE FOUND
By: Meltez Smith

Woe to my ears fell words soft lovely full of delight.

And before my eyes stood the queen I hear, she loves me true and she loves me right.

Sweet encouragable you our fights we fight.

Up against the battle of two fought as one we fight.

Kiss my lips taste victory court me now make history.

Beautiful queen walk before me, give us this chance to make a story.

Let all of our past be fuel to fire.

And presently seek to know you I admire.

This is the chance I've dreamed to see.

You and I happy oh shall we be.

The apple of grace such envy we.

Dwell in my heart and straight on my mind.

You've found a real man so come be mine…

Unspoken Voices From The Darkest Of Races

By: Meltez Smith

We who spoke before are the black unnamed. No color is the core of the person you blamed. You see I am the poor considered as the lame. Dressed in humble attire coming yet out of shame.

But my actions are loud and my voice speaks real. Impress upon many a crowd choose the life yet I'll yield. With awesome greatfulness I'm glad who else could hold in so much pain.

The Lord has blessed with all I have the rest in life bears my name. Significant change a vision sought just to provide an average man. My footsteps move sometimes get caught my goal yet shine to light the plan

Seeing the fruit of my labor span. Out to such reaches to give and hand. Blessed of the Lord I must share whats grand. This is the joy that dwells in my heart. Though not yet there faith unfolds the art.

Of what much patience and sufferings bring. Through countless visions called only dreams. I'm held in awe inspired still. This gap unclosed one day will fill. In whatever manner is upon God's will…

World's Greatest Gift LOVE
By: Meltez Smith

Search for my heart is true beautiful love is in my sight

Not far out of my grasp of reach let me touch you if I just might

Darling of all my world revolves whatever would I do without. The thought of never seeing you again who would dare to even talk about

If everyone in the world hates you then here is one who does not

For what I see is so special and none can ever replace what I have got

You see the missing link for what I live is filled in tears. The offspring of my genes have made my heart so glad with cheers

Two people never forgotten special ones I ever adore

You guessed it my wonderful parents may I one day even the score

Worked so hard for me to obtain don't ever question what they are for. As life passes us by may they know the root of my love to the core

And many others whom we hold dear embrace them while you can

Look I tell you my friend for those close you are a fan

The biggest yet they should ever see for no one else cares like you

The greatest majority in numbers we talk still remain in portions that are few

Be a witness that can attest love is all for you…

Where Faith Resides
By: Meltez Smith

Living life with uncertain sight. Passionate treasures all held so tight. Who are you and just where do you stand. For love of all is entirely at hand. Enough about greatness let us humbly accept. Each person we meet with arms stretched out to help. Recognize life and the purpose we obtain. Recognize colors are people of the same. For peace in this way is not found great and true. but now is the day for peace makers to do. For we are the few who take part in this race. Among the old and new all colors in one place. As we live among wishes being driven by dreams. Through faith we pitched it all the way as it seems. For the cause and endeavors is so dear to our heart. Fought with unpleasure battled by the smart. Uncertain is this life and for granted not taken. Unsteady is this fight so proper tools we are making. And fitting for that day when our memories shall dwell. In the roles we play and the life we held.

Your Beliefs Are Not All Mine
By: Meltez Smith

Father of all ruler and prince, the only one to break the barrier and fence

You say your atheist well that I respect, but don't knock me for God I respect

You say you're gay well that is your choice, that way of life on me you never can force

You murder and steal and that is your pleasure, the government does the same a role model to measure

Stop the violence and stop the hate, give to the Americans a life of good fate

We are all people related by blood, with flesh and bones that return to the mud

There is none or any of us who is great, I strongly emphasize this truth I must state

Look not down on people for who they are, look not down on people for what they do

Remember that time is not far, for reaping day is nothing new…

Your Encouragement Is Life To Me
By: Meltez Smith

Just bless and curse me not seen is the struggle of a poor man being fought

In the light of shame peace and hunger is brought

To the table of grace spread is ambition to be sought

Through perilous times we come to nought

For salvation of hope in the class to be caught

Scattered as treasures with great value comes a cost

Preach as many lectures love is temporary until our loss

Just bless and curse me not the day of deliverance brings joy and joy we spot

From turmoil and ashes we are found so hot

With our unusual demeanor we are sought out to be got

Bringing forth old making history new

Remember in the last days we are found and still true…

The Essence Of Love

By: Meltez Smith

Let me rewind this chapter to bring my love to a close. Your sweet compassionate face has filled my heart with a rose. What grace you've found in my eyesight and not by deeds alone. But by the one I've come to know my feelings are already known. Whether destiny coincidense or just out of the blue, the grounds we tread are deep. And I don't care what others say our love we only can keep. For what has brought us together is what can only maintain. And if we don't succeed upon who will it be a strain. As I speak profoundly of to whom I decree. The message is so very clear only she can offer a plea. Not based on circumstances this is the one I've chosen. It has not put me in a steady state of a mentality that is frozen. For better or worse and rich or poor are vowels to be taken sincere. Only the two being joined together can be the ones to adhere. Everyone else can speculate and assume whatever they like. As the two embarke on a journey they must be on a constant strike. To let those in dought see that wow their love is true. And totally ignore the ones that say it's just yet not through…

Money Defines not Greatness
By: Meltez Smith

Undertaking time is yet but what we define, with no riches of pleasure we are left ill and behind

Still under pressure how we shine, though thoughts to succeed are out of mind

We have the hearts to be clever scrutinizing charts for human measure

We have the love that amounts whatever being chastened to keep our goals together

We find no end to what true love treasures and this is our reign that speaks forever

Oh how through much we came and have still far to go you see a life mixed in shame I see one set to blow

Where enemies have set hurdles and even bashed great egos

Through demonizing our swept character our humble grace is never lost

We will bring another form to bear with care and be vigil to the cross…

One God Eternally Great Forever
By: Meltez Smith

From black til morning does the dawn appeal, affixed are rays from its bright light to show

A brand new day fixed by the power of his will, the Lord mighty forever reigns on his subjects below

Caught by his talents oh praise him all, ye who are alive witness his power be known

From now and forever is his blessedness to all, his grace and mercy being yet now even shown

Wonders rest with the questions why? A GOD so powerful holds in man esteem

Is it to be more than his pleasure that we seek to know why

The LORD sovereign and mighty held to be great is ever seen

So thus dwells our portion in light of today, choosing to make GOD our life we give

To him we entrust with our lives to obey, the cause of our debt bears in faith to GOD we live…

Make Life To Be The Most You Can

By: Meltez Smith

Respect I the story of life's future end, a cycle repeating to no avail is a man strong to win

So why do we live this life as though yet it's uncursed, never are we taken unaware of our blatant sinful deeds

For this is our time to act for good as our life is unrehearsed, never to say that oh I would for time does come and speeds

Our vastness of life that dwells by thought in everything that we perceive

Whether good or bad is our intention brought and who just speaks to be nieve

Oh if time would come to pass our treacherous ways, so in the end we could be found without blame

Upon the lives of those who our memory displays, is the role we lead held by the life we aim…

No Other Like You
By: Meltez Smith

Close your eyes and look and see, that's where imagination can start and be

We all have wishes we hope could come true, fantasies are ok but don't get so blue

Richness only last for a while, no matter what you say you can't die in style

Live the life of luxury, despise the poor, tell me who you always think is wanting more

I have many faces none of the which you'll understand, switching them by the challenges and every situation at hand

Oh don't you flip out, you know you have many faces to, like on the job, at home, just simply being you

We switch them so often and realize it not, with everything life brings us new techniques we adopt

Like wildebeest in thrive on the sarangetti, our strategy develops as the almighty holds it steady

In what direction we choose we really don't know, relying on our best instincts and going with the flow

So in this wild world of imagination, let's keep our heads on straight and avoid frustration…

Never Dought Speak Positive

By: Meltez Smith

Faith in advance what speaks to believe, upon GOD'S will I advance from the hurt that I grieve

Look on others now to enhance a good life and relieve

From the time that I struggled from the fear that I hid, from the tears that came doubled from the pain that I lived

Irreplaceable joy has marked its stake in its place, a long time coming none the less joy is the meat of I taste

Where the weeping hearted cry and mourn from the spoils of disgrace

Forever in my heart and sworn to the ones that do face

To touch and help as many abroad as the LORD will provide, never ever will I just forget

For the LORD has been my guide…

Show Love Regardless Of What You Contend With

By: Meltez Smith

Ever before have you seen past or felt great

Company alone with whom you share is that just way past to late

At some point there's a bridge that will stay strong or collapse

Hold tight fit or perish together is a relationship maybe perhaps

Seen by many who don't know what's real all closed behind doors are traps

Laid out by guilt lies and ill feelings kept, that longs for change hate and grief entraps

To see stress uplifted burdens not gone but light

In these arms of love come and behold the gifted, let me be myself day and night

As a witness share know true love is there

A relationship built more than upon care

Dismiss my love is to fall deep in despair, I am one and truly of the rare…

www.ingramcontent.com/pod-product-compliance
Lightning Source LLC
Chambersburg PA
CBHW071503070526
44578CB00001B/431